AF598734

TO:

FROM:

DATE:

Christian art gifts®

The LORD is my *light* and my *salvation*. Ps. 27:1

"All things are *possible* with God." Mark 10:27

I can do all this through Him who gives me *strength*. Phil. 4:13

Mercy, peace and *love* be yours in abundance. Jude 1:2

"Be *still*, and know that I am God." Ps. 46:10

Every good and *perfect* gift is from above. James 1:17

"Where your *treasure* is, there your *heart* will be also." Matt. 6:21

If anything is *excellent or praiseworthy* – *think* about such things. Phil. 4:8

God...does great things *beyond* our *understanding.* Job 37:5

Give *thanks* to the LORD, for He is good; His *love* endures *forever*. Ps. 118:29

Trust in the LORD with all your heart. Prov. 3:5

I will *sing* the LORD's *praise,* for He has been good to me. Ps. 13:6

Great are the *works* of the LORD. Ps. 111:2

"I am the *way* and the *truth* and the *life*." John 14:6

Be *joyful* in hope, *patient* in affliction, *faithful* in prayer. Rom. 12:12

"*Rejoice* and be glad, because great is your reward in *heaven*." Matt. 5:12

"*Everything* is possible for one who *believes*." Mark 9:23

Let us *love* one another, for love comes from God. 1 John 4:7

Let the *peace* of Christ rule in your *hearts.* Col. 3:15

The LORD is *near*...to all who call on Him in *truth*. Ps. 145:18

Truly my soul finds *rest* in God. Ps. 62:1

The LORD your God will *bless* you...in all the work of your *hands*. Deut. 16:15

"My *Presence* will go with you, and I will give you ***rest.***" Ex. 33:14

The Lord is my *light* and my *salvation*. Ps. 27:1

"All things are *possible* with God." Mark 10:27

I can do all this through Him who gives me *strength*. Phil. 4:13

Mercy, peace and *love* be yours in abundance. Jude 1:2

"Be *still*, and know that I am God." Ps. 46:10

Every good and *perfect* gift is from above. James 1:17

"Where your *treasure* is, there your *heart* will be also." Matt. 6:21

If anything is *excellent or praiseworthy* – *think* about such things. Phil. 4:8

God...does great things *beyond* our *understanding.* Job 37:5

Give *thanks* to the LORD, for He is good; His *love* endures *forever*. Ps. 118:29

Trust in the LORD with all your heart. Prov. 3:5

I will *sing* the LORD's *praise*, for He has been good to me. Ps. 13:6

Great are the ***works*** of the LORD. Ps. 111:2

The LORD will *guide* you always. Isa. 58:11

"I am the *way* and the *truth* and the *life*." John 14:6

Be *joyful* in hope, *patient* in affliction, *faithful* in prayer. Rom. 12:12

"*Rejoice* and be glad, because great is your reward in *heaven*." Matt. 5:12

"*Everything* is possible for one who *believes*." Mark 9:23

Let us *love* one another, for love comes from God. 1 John 4:7

Let the *peace* of Christ rule in your *hearts.* Col. 3:15

The Lord is *near*...to all who call on Him in *truth*. Ps. 145:18

Truly my soul finds *rest* in God. Ps. 62:1

The LORD your God will *bless* you...in all the work of your *hands*. Deut. 16:15

"My *Presence* will go with you, and I will give you ***rest***." Ex. 33:14

The LORD is my *light* and my *salvation*. Ps. 27:1

"All things are *possible* with God." Mark 10:27

I can do all this through Him who gives me *strength*. Phil. 4:13

Mercy, peace and *love* be yours in abundance. Jude 1:2

"Be *still*, and know that I am God." Ps. 46:10

Every good and *perfect* gift is from above. James 1:17

"Where your *treasure* is, there your *heart* will be also." Matt. 6:21

If anything is *excellent or praiseworthy* – *think* about such things. Phil. 4:8

God...does great things *beyond* our *understanding.* Job 37:5

Give *thanks* to the LORD, for He is good; His *love* endures *forever.* Ps. 118:29

Trust in the LORD with all your heart. Prov. 3:5

I will *sing* the LORD's *praise,* for He has been good to me. Ps. 13:6

Great are the ***works*** of the LORD. Ps. 111:2

The LORD will *guide* you always. Isa. 58:11

"I am the *way* and the *truth* and the *life*." John 14:6

Be *joyful* in hope, *patient* in affliction, *faithful* in prayer. Rom. 12:12

"*Rejoice* and be glad, because great is your reward in *heaven*." Matt. 5:12

"*Everything* is possible for one who *believes*." Mark 9:23

Let us *love* one another, for love comes from God. 1 John 4:7

Let the *peace* of Christ rule in your *hearts.* Col. 3:15

The LORD is *near*...to all who call on Him in *truth*. Ps. 145:18

Truly my soul finds *rest* in God. Ps. 62:1

The LORD your God will *bless* you...in all the work of your *hands*. Deut. 16:15

"My *Presence* will go with you, and I will give you ***rest***." Ex. 33:14

The LORD is my *light* and my *salvation*. Ps. 27:1

"All things are *possible* with God." Mark 10:27

I can do all this through Him who gives me *strength*. Phil. 4:13

Mercy, peace and *love* be yours in abundance. Jude 1:2

"Be *still*, and know that I am God." Ps. 46:10

Every good and *perfect* gift is from above. James 1:17

"Where your *treasure* is, there your *heart* will be also." Matt. 6:21

If anything is *excellent or praiseworthy* – *think* about such things. Phil. 4:8

God...does great things *beyond* our *understanding.* Job 37:5

Give *thanks* to the LORD, for He is good; His *love* endures *forever*. Ps. 118:29

Trust in the LORD with all your heart. Prov. 3:5

I will *sing* the LORD's *praise,* for He has been good to me. Ps. 13:6

Great are the *works* of the LORD. Ps. 111:2

The LORD will *guide* you always. Isa. 58:11

"I am the *way* and the *truth* and the *life*." John 14:6

Be *joyful* in hope, *patient* in affliction, *faithful* in prayer. Rom. 12:12

"*Rejoice* and be glad, because great is your reward in *heaven*." Matt. 5:12

"*Everything* is possible for one who *believes*." Mark 9:23

Let us *love* one another, for love comes from God. 1 John 4:7

Let the *peace* of Christ rule in your *hearts.* Col. 3:15

The LORD is *near*...to all who call on Him in *truth*. Ps. 145:18

Truly my soul finds *rest* in God. Ps. 62:1

The LORD your God will *bless* you...in all the work of your *hands*. Deut. 16:15

"My *Presence* will go with you, and I will give you ***rest.***" Ex. 33:14

The LORD is my *light* and my *salvation*. Ps. 27:1

"All things are *possible* with God." Mark 10:27

I can do all this through Him who gives me *strength*. Phil. 4:13

Mercy, peace and *love* be yours in abundance. Jude 1:2

"Be *still*, and know that I am God." Ps. 46:10

Every good and *perfect* gift is from above. James 1:17

"Where your *treasure* is, there your *heart* will be also." Matt. 6:21

God...does great things *beyond* our *understanding.* Job 37:5

Give *thanks* to the LORD, for He is good; His *love* endures *forever*. Ps. 118:29

Trust in the LORD with all your heart. Prov. 3:5

I will *sing* the LORD's *praise,* for He has been good to me. Ps. 13:6

Great are the *works* of the LORD. Ps. 111:2

The LORD will *guide* you always. Isa. 58:11

"I am the *way* and the *truth* and the *life*." John 14:6

Be *joyful* in hope, *patient* in affliction, *faithful* in prayer. Rom. 12:12

"*Rejoice* and be glad, because great is your reward in *heaven*." Matt. 5:12

"*Everything* is possible for one who *believes*." Mark 9:23

Let us *love* one another, for love comes from God. 1 John 4:7

Let the *peace* of Christ rule in your *hearts.* Col. 3:15

The LORD is *near*...to all who call on Him in *truth*. Ps. 145:18

Truly my soul finds *rest* in God. Ps. 62:1

The LORD your God will *bless* you...in all the work of your *hands*. Deut. 16:15

"My *Presence* will go with you, and I will give you ***rest***." Ex. 33:14

The LORD is my *light* and my *salvation*. Ps. 27:1

"All things are *possible* with God." Mark 10:27

I can do all this through Him who gives me *strength*. Phil. 4:13

Mercy, peace and *love* be yours in abundance. Jude 1:2

"Be *still*, and know that I am God." Ps. 46:10

Every good and *perfect* gift is from above. James 1:17

"Where your *treasure* is, there your *heart* will be also." Matt. 6:21

If anything is *excellent or praiseworthy* – *think* about such things. Phil. 4:8

God...does great things *beyond* our *understanding.* Job 37:5

Give *thanks* to the LORD, for He is good; His *love* endures *forever*. Ps. 118:29

Trust in the LORD with all your heart. Prov. 3:5

I will *sing* the LORD's *praise,* for He has been good to me. Ps. 13:6

Great are the ***works*** of the LORD. Ps. 111:2

The Lord will *guide* you always. Isa. 58:11

"I am the *way* and the *truth* and the *life*." John 14:6

Be *joyful* in hope, *patient* in affliction, *faithful* in prayer. Rom. 12:12

"*Rejoice* and be glad, because great is your reward in *heaven*." Matt. 5:12

"*Everything* is possible for one who *believes*." Mark 9:23

Let us *love* one another, for love comes from God. 1 John 4:7

Let the *peace* of Christ rule in your *hearts.* Col. 3:15

The Lord is *near*...to all who call on Him in *truth*. Ps. 145:18

Truly my soul finds *rest* in God. Ps. 62:1

The LORD your God will *bless* you...in all the work of your *hands*. Deut. 16:15

"My *Presence* will go with you, and I will give you ***rest.***" Ex. 33:14

The LORD is my *light* and my *salvation*. Ps. 27:1

"All things are *possible* with God." Mark 10:27

I can do all this through Him who gives me *strength*. Phil. 4:13

Mercy, peace and *love* be yours in abundance. Jude 1:2

"Be *still*, and know that I am God." Ps. 46:10

Every good and *perfect* gift is from above. James 1:17

"Where your *treasure* is, there your *heart* will be also." Matt. 6:21

If anything is *excellent or praiseworthy* – *think* about such things. Phil. 4:8

God...does great things *beyond* our *understanding.* Job 37:5

Give *thanks* to the LORD, for He is good; His *love* endures *forever*. Ps. 118:29

Trust in the LORD with all your heart. Prov. 3:5

I will *sing* the LORD's *praise,* for He has been good to me. Ps. 13:6

Great are the *works* of the LORD. Ps. 111:2

The Lord will *guide* you always. Isa. 58:11

"I am the *way* and the *truth* and the *life*." John 14:6

Be *joyful* in hope, *patient* in affliction, *faithful* in prayer. Rom. 12:12

"*Rejoice* and be glad, because great is your reward in *heaven*." Matt. 5:12

"*Everything* is possible for one who ***believes***." Mark 9:23

Let us *love* one another, for love comes from God. 1 John 4:7

Let the *peace* of Christ rule in your *hearts.* Col. 3:15

The LORD is *near*...to all who call on Him in *truth*. Ps. 145:18

Truly my soul finds *rest* in God. Ps. 62:1

The LORD your God will *bless* you...in all the work of your *hands*. Deut. 16:15

"My *Presence* will go with you, and I will give you ***rest***." Ex. 33:14

The LORD is my *light* and my *salvation*. Ps. 27:1

"All things are *possible* with God." Mark 10:27

I can do all this through Him who gives me *strength*. Phil. 4:13

Mercy, peace and *love* be yours in abundance. Jude 1:2

"Be *still*, and know that I am God." Ps. 46:10

Every good and *perfect* gift is from above. James 1:17

"Where your *treasure* is, there your *heart* will be also." Matt. 6:21

If anything is *excellent or praiseworthy* – *think* about such things. Phil. 4:8

God...does great things *beyond* our *understanding.* Job 37:5

Give *thanks* to the LORD, for He is good; His *love* endures *forever*. Ps. 118:29

Trust in the LORD with all your heart. Prov. 3:5

I will *sing* the LORD's *praise,* for He has been good to me. Ps. 13:6

Great are the *works* of the LORD. Ps. 111:2

The LORD will *guide* you always. Isa. 58:11

"I am the *way* and the *truth* and the *life*." John 14:6

Be *joyful* in hope, *patient* in affliction, *faithful* in prayer. Rom. 12:12

"*Rejoice* and be glad, because great is your reward in *heaven*." Matt. 5:12

"*Everything* is possible for one who *believes*." Mark 9:23

Let us *love* one another, for love comes from God. 1 John 4:7

Let the *peace* of Christ rule in your *hearts.* Col. 3:15

The LORD is *near*...to all who call on Him in *truth*. Ps. 145:18

Truly my soul finds *rest* in God. Ps. 62:1

The LORD your God will *bless* you...in all the work of your *hands*. Deut. 16:15

"My *Presence* will go with you, and I will give you ***rest***." Ex. 33:14

The LORD is my *light* and my *salvation*. Ps. 27:1

"All things are *possible* with God." Mark 10:27

I can do all this through Him who gives me *strength*. Phil. 4:13

Mercy, peace and *love* be yours in abundance. Jude 1:2

"Be *still*, and know that I am God." Ps. 46:10

Every good and *perfect* gift is from above. James 1:17

"Where your *treasure* is, there your *heart* will be also." Matt. 6:21

If anything is *excellent or praiseworthy* – *think* about such things. Phil. 4:8

God...does great things *beyond* our *understanding.* Job 37:5

Give *thanks* to the LORD, for He is good; His *love* endures *forever.* Ps. 118:29

Trust in the LORD with all your heart. Prov. 3:5

I will *sing* the LORD's *praise,* for He has been good to me. Ps. 13:6

Great are the *works* of the LORD. Ps. 111:2

The LORD will *guide* you always. Isa. 58:11

"I am the *way* and the *truth* and the *life*." John 14:6

Be *joyful* in hope, *patient* in affliction, *faithful* in prayer. Rom. 12:12

"*Rejoice* and be glad, because great is your reward in *heaven*." Matt. 5:12

"*Everything* is possible for one who *believes*." Mark 9:23

Let us *love* one another, for love comes from God. 1 John 4:7

Let the *peace* of Christ rule in your *hearts.* Col. 3:15

The LORD is *near*...to all who call on Him in *truth*. Ps. 145:18

Truly my soul finds *rest* in God. Ps. 62:1

The LORD your God will *bless* you...in all the work of your *hands.* Deut. 16:15

"My *Presence* will go with you, and I will give you ***rest***." Ex. 33:14

The LORD is my *light* and my *salvation*. Ps. 27:1

"All things are *possible* with God." Mark 10:27

I can do all this through Him who gives me *strength*. Phil. 4:13

Mercy, peace and *love* be yours in abundance. Jude 1:2

"Be *still*, and know that I am God." Ps. 46:10

Every good and *perfect* gift is from above. James 1:17

"Where your *treasure* is, there your *heart* will be also." Matt. 6:21

If anything is *excellent or praiseworthy* – *think* about such things. Phil. 4:8

God...does great things *beyond* our *understanding.* Job 37:5

Give *thanks* to the LORD, for He is good; His *love* endures *forever*. Ps. 118:29

Trust in the LORD with all your heart. Prov. 3:5

I will *sing* the LORD's *praise,* for He has been good to me. Ps. 13:6

The LORD will *guide* you always. Isa. 58:11

"I am the *way* and the *truth* and the *life*." John 14:6

Be *joyful* in hope, *patient* in affliction, *faithful* in prayer. Rom. 12:12

"*Rejoice* and be glad, because great is your reward in *heaven*." Matt. 5:12

"*Everything* is possible for one who *believes*." Mark 9:23

Let us *love* one another, for love comes from God. 1 John 4:7

Let the *peace* of Christ rule in your *hearts.* Col. 3:15

The LORD is *near*...to all who call on Him in *truth*. Ps. 145:18

Truly my soul finds *rest* in God. Ps. 62:1

The Lord your God will *bless* you...in all the work of your *hands*. Deut. 16:15

"My *Presence* will go with you, and I will give you *rest*." Ex. 33:14

The LORD is my *light* and my *salvation*. Ps. 27:1

"All things are *possible* with God." Mark 10:27

I can do all this through Him who gives me *strength*. Phil. 4:13

Mercy, peace and *love* be yours in abundance. Jude 1:2

"Be *still*, and know that I am God." Ps. 46:10

Every good and *perfect* gift is from above. James 1:17

"Where your *treasure* is, there your *heart* will be also." Matt. 6:21

If anything is *excellent or praiseworthy* – *think* about such things. Phil. 4:8

God...does great things *beyond* our *understanding.* Job 37:5

Give *thanks* to the LORD, for He is good; His *love* endures *forever*. Ps. 118:29

Trust in the LORD with all your heart. Prov. 3:5

I will *sing* the LORD's *praise,* for He has been good to me. Ps. 13:6

Great are the ***works*** of the LORD. Ps. 111:2

The LORD will *guide* you always. Isa. 58:11

"I am the *way* and the *truth* and the *life*." John 14:6

Be *joyful* in hope, *patient* in affliction, *faithful* in prayer. Rom. 12:12

"*Rejoice* and be glad, because great is your reward in *heaven*." Matt. 5:12

"*Everything* is possible for one who *believes*." Mark 9:23

Let us *love* one another, for love comes from God. 1 John 4:7

Let the *peace* of Christ rule in your *hearts.* Col. 3:15

Truly my soul finds *rest* in God. Ps. 62:1

The LORD your God will *bless* you...in all the work of your *hands*. Deut. 16:15

"My *Presence* will go with you, and I will give you ***rest.***" Ex. 33:14

The LORD is my *light* and my *salvation*. Ps. 27:1

"All things are *possible* with God." Mark 10:27

I can do all this through Him who gives me *strength*. Phil. 4:13

Mercy, peace and *love* be yours in abundance. Jude 1:2

"Be *still*, and know that I am God." Ps. 46:10

Every good and *perfect* gift is from above. James 1:17

"Where your *treasure* is, there your *heart* will be also." Matt. 6:21

God...does great things *beyond* our *understanding.* Job 37:5

Give *thanks* to the LORD, for He is good; His *love* endures *forever*. Ps. 118:29

Trust in the LORD with all your heart. Prov. 3:5

I will *sing* the LORD's *praise,* for He has been good to me. Ps. 13:6

Great are the ***works*** of the LORD. Ps. 111:2

The LORD will *guide* you always. Isa. 58:11

“I am the *way* and the *truth* and the *life*.” John 14:6

Be *joyful* in hope, *patient* in affliction, *faithful* in prayer. Rom. 12:12

"*Rejoice* and be glad, because great is your reward in *heaven*." Matt. 5:12

"*Everything* is possible for one who ***believes***." Mark 9:23

Let us *love* one another, for love comes from God. 1 John 4:7

Let the *peace* of Christ rule in your *hearts.* Col. 3:15

The LORD is *near*...to all who call on Him in *truth*. Ps. 145:18

Truly my soul finds *rest* in God. Ps. 62:1